TKO

A Lost Night in Tokyo

Scott Shaw

Buddha Rose Publications

TKO: A Lost Night in Tokyo

First Edition 1989
Second Edition 2010

ISBN: 1-877792-08-X
ISBN-13: 9781877792083

Library of Congress
Cataloging in Publication Data:
Shaw, Scott
TKO: A Lost Night in Tokyo
1. Tokyo (Japan) – Poetry
2. I. Title
PS3568.H38627T56 1989
811' .54 – dc20

Library of Congress Catalog Card Number:
89-23919

10 9 8 7 6 5 4 3 2 1

Printed in the United States of America

TKO

A Lost Night in Tokyo

contents

one

have you left yourself
a moment to dream

a moment to dream
as the world falls down around you

have you left yourself
a moment of illusion

a moment of illusion
in a room far too small

cast away the demons
the demon that inhabit
the world in which we live

hand to me the elixir
in a world of fading fantasies

for the vision it gives
is so much more pure

slap me with your vision
slap me with your sound
slap me with your omnipresence
as you let your dream take me down

fill me with your egotism
fill me with your style
fill me up
slam me hard
how I love it
you know, how I love it so

three

a dream in a darken alley
a dream in the late night
a dream
it is all and still the same

the air is cold, old
her perfume
passes by me
in a world passing by me

    I have been touched
    yes, I have been touched
    I know the feeling

    yet in this land of pleasure
    the embrace it has escaped me
    evaded me thus far

    as this night of intoxication
    begins to take hold

it is the world
of the elixir
the world
where fluid gives birth to the realm

    where nothing need be spoken
    yet everything is said

where nothing really matters
yet everything be known

it is in this world
that I exist

I make my retreat
into this drunken paradise

escape the feeling of
nothingness
escape to the feeling of
nothingness

the same word
but the meanings
they are lifetimes apart

escape from somewhere
escape to nowhere

where the absence of
the missing touch
no longer has any validity
and everything
means nothing at all

all the pleasure
all the pain

all the conquest
all the dreams

I have become unburdened
yes, I am now free
in this losing battle
of a warrior constantly in flight

four

dancing in the obvious
I always show them how to drink
dancing *en route* to the oblivions
I always show them how to pound

dancing in this obsession
is there ever any other way
dancing in this obliteration
I throw a kiss to the goddess
I throw a kiss to the night
a kiss to the aloneness
but it is a kiss
just the same

five

the Japanese hooker
sitting down the bar
no,
she just doesn't appreciate style

I sit here
pounding hard
mega big time

my feelings
they have become numb

and the casual whore
sitting midway
she checks out an Aussie
ordering a stout

he is clad
in his short hair
his cheap suit
ordering a cheap beer

I sit here
my hair – long and California blonde
my clothing – long and baggy
European by manufacture and design

but the obvious
forever seems to call the fool

the sub-cultured
is only heard
by the ears of a few

so I give you my best
listen and pay all you will
the dream of another nighttime
is coming on fast
where the dreams will live
the stylish will rule
and the fashion/passion
will never take its toll

the Japanese
hooker
sitting down the bar
no, she just doesn't appreciate style

six

he has got his moral
the guy sitting down the bar
me, I have nothing

no wife
no children
no fear of AIDS

nothing left to lose
just a still hard dream
in a night subdued against the wisdom
rubber hard against the fantasy

yes, I am a drunk
yes, I am a mystic
isn't it all the same

plastered hard
against the wall of reality
pasted here
within the confines of a dream

with nothing left to lose
nothing left to gain

the music in this bar
plays on and on
dipped too long

like an oreo cookie
in sour milk

    no pain
    no gain
    so I have heard

I could be anywhere
but here and alone is where I am

so I drill another one
for the ole' gipper
I hammer one
for the night
I pound one
for no reason at all
I lose myself
in the six and a half ways to dream

    crying all alone
    the passion and the purpose
    of all the mystics
    of all the ages
    of all the times

so this bar
it proves to be unenlightening
as the words drunkenly scribble
upon this written page

so I kiss the night
I kiss the dream of passion
I throw a kiss
to a unoccupied midway hooker
and I just try to forget

the bad music it plays on
me, I choose to walk away
walk to a place
where there are others
who have no fear

no fear
no morals
metaphysics in the making
and love for the taking

seven

the poet cries
as he awaits the arrival
of the drunken poetic dream

it is ten to twelve
the witching hour
is almost upon us

the music it is bullshit
bullshit straight out
of the Philippines

the singer sings bullshit
and I
the perfect drunken poet
sits here and dream

for me
I have just arrived
the perfect poet
the perfect drunken poet
the perfect drunkenness
has just come upon me

lost in the sin
lost in the drink
lost where the mind runs free

the words run free

there are no bounds
to tie me down

yes
the perfect poet
has arrives

are you here alone
alone on a holiday
I hear someone say to me

I say nothing

alone on a Saturday night ?
questions, I hear them again

Saturday, it must be Saturday
but everyday is Saturday to me

live with me
in ancient wisdom
live with me
the breath of this day

everyday is Saturday
promise me forever
as the drink
slowly goes down

drunk and alone
so I am again
funny how it always seems
to turn out that way

ah, the bastions of poetry
the dreams of a drunk
the wisdom of the fools
and the scribes of a heretic

and for all those
who cling to the rhythm
all those
who live in the clan of the night
and for all those
who think they are
what they never are
dream on
dream on
dream/scream

alone and in Asia
here I am again
out on the outskirts
it may just as well be Tibet

Tibet, where I was three months ago

yes, it could be anywhere

but Tokyo is where I am
lost in the drunken
lost in the obscene
rambling to no one's ears
as some horrible music
plays on

> you know
> I have forever wondered
> how things so bad
> appear to be so good
> is it just for the minds
> of the unthinking
> those who believe the lies
> the lie of
> where is here is right
> is it just for the fools
> fools who have never
> drunkenly screams
> in a lost and lonely
> Asian night

yes, it could be any dream
for any dream will do
but the black of the night
it calls me out
it screams at me

come here
come here

so I ask for my bar bill
I ask for it in Japanese

no, I am not too drunk
to speak the tongue

the bartender he looks at me
yeah, I know
I could stay here all night
he knows that I have done it before
but the bad music plays on and on
and the dream of the goddess
well…
she cries so loudly to me
while she softly whispers my name

I hear
come to me
come to me
come to me

eight

I stagger to my room
in oblivion
I stagger to my room
but I am alone
I stagger to my room
in pure *pointblank* shape
it is so empty

no hooker in front of me
no lover to my side
no disco dolly
to watch over me

    nothing
    nothing
    it is so poetic

is it my attitude
that keeps me separate
allows me to remain
lost in the night
is it the ramblings of a fool
the promises of a preacher
or the prostitution of a priest
that leaves me no alternative
but to turn right
at the far side of midnight
    asylum
    poetic asylum

where the words are written
the dreams
and the lies created

life
it can only be truly lived
by the mystics

life
it is only truly known
by the drunk

life
with its never ending installments
of posers
and promisers
liars and fools

words
they are all spoken
time
it all is spent
and left
is only the few noted moments
worth nothing
to no one
but the self

listen with dancing ears…

nine

why should I pretend to live
any other dream
when this one
it is so real

I cry for the longing
the longing and the love
I cry like any messiah
any other dreamer
for the desire
of no desire

    but the desire
    it remains just the same

so I will walk the streets
like the healers
like the hookers
like the pure
and the fools

I will walk in my drunken passion
my passion of the night
my passion for the night
my passion that waits to be fulfilled

ten

as I walk
drunken
in the Tokyo winter night
fuck becomes the word
the word
repeated in my mind

    fuck
    the world
    fuck
    the female form
    fuck this
    and fuck that

fuck
the vocabulary
of a drunkard

eleven

I am intoxicated
        beyond belief
fucked up
in any other diction

I approach the elevator
of my five star hotel
the name of which
for all intensive purposes
shall remain nameless

        I stagger
        I fall into the wall
        I await
        await the arrival
        of my transportation
        transportation to lobby level
        ground level
        transportation to the street(s)
        flirtation with the street

        awaiting

I want out
I want one thing
one thing only in mind
        contact
        drunken contact
        with that of the opposite sex

but I must chill
I must remain in wait
remain
standing tall
remain
in all the remainingness
for I must exit the front doors
of my ever known
I am ever well known
hotel
in the Tokyo skyline
yes, I must chill

chill down
chill down
stand up straight
don’t fall

twelve

drunk
yes, I am
but no,
I am no fool

I left my wallet
my credit cards
in my room

room 3806
is you please

I left my wallet
My credit cards
I took some spending cash
to buy my way to paradise
I took some balloons of privilege
to protect my inner working
and I took
my mini tape recorder
which into now
I do
drunkenly speak

thirteen

it is cold outside
and I hear a siren call

do you hear it
can you hear it

it passes by me
in all its eloquence

I walk
there they are
the call of my dream
the calling of the night
two women
good women
nice women
they wait for a taxi
a taxi home
to their shelter
a taxi home
to their forbidden safety

can they believe
that it really exists

I could tell them
that I love them
would they ever believe

my words
could they ever see through
my illusion
and offer me
passive peace
in a faltering mystical life

or I could tell them
that I simply want to fuck them
perhaps
they may understand that
far more

for truth
it is blatant
lies
they are so surreal
and in the end
all that matters
is the nothing
that we all come to feel

it is so cold out tonight
as I drunkenly walk the streets

fourteen

somebody must have died
in the bar that I was in
the ambulance
pulls up front
pulls of center

it could have been me
it probably was

this is all a ghost's illusion
a midnight tall tale
me
walking out into the night

what finer a way to go
go to where there is never anymore

what a finer way to fade
fade to gray

there is certainly
no more perfect way to go
to the paradise
of the dreamers

the Shangri-La
of the poets

all of them drunkards
just like me

drunk and dead

god, I am fucked up

and dead men
tell no tales

fifteen

here comes a woman
walking my direction
        my direction
        in the opposite direction

        let me play it cool
        let me play it suave

footsteps
they pass
they pass
at a calculated distance

I guess I must have staggered
for she walked way
out of my way

well hey
if she don't want to know
then forget her

walk on
a little bit farther
a little bit deeper
into the night

sixteen

the wind is blowing
Tokyo's winter confronts me
confounds me
pounds on me

        through my long coat
        through my drunkenness
        through my loneliness

it is only a fool's cry
        from eternity
        into maturity

        a subject
        which I never understood

        a reason
        which I never found a reason for

give me this dream
I have desired it
give me this desire
I have dreamed of it

drunken poetics
and the enclosing winter night
of Tokyo

the police
they lay in wait
across the street from me
in wait
for anther type of criminal
other than I

a drunken functional being
not a drunken dysfunction literate

literature being the only pose

I have lived it
I am living it
may it never be
any other way

bring on the cold
I have ordered it
bring on the night
I have purchased it
bring on the dream
for I have paid dearly for it

seventeen

sex
yes
I want sex

desire
yes
it is
        just another desire

desire to be yearned for
desire to die for
desire be required

        desire
        just the same

Jesus
he had a desire
make people believe
that he was
who he said he was

                quiet men
                never become saints

the Buddha
he had a desire
the desire of no desire

desire
just the same

me
well
I too have a desire
this moment/this night
it is as good as any other night

no
I am not pretending
no
I am not lying
no
I am not saying
it is anything
but what it is

DESIRE

eighteen

twenty-nine
and oh so fine
by thirty
I want to be a millionaire

age comes on
age comes down
time
it flies away to nowhere

love and lust
powers are lost and gained
give me another reason
any reason will do just fine

where is the princess
to caress my life
an Asian, Tokyo Goddess
who offers me lost loving dreams
in a cold and freezing
drunken night

served in an after-hours dish
where any dream will do

love is lust
fire at will
point the gun at me
and shoot to kill

nineteen

taxis
they do light the night

moving to a profound rhythm
unheard by the uninitiated
unknown to the dwellers
of the aft-world
they are the veins
they are the unstopping
they are the blood flow
they are life
in a world
that slowly grows silent
with each assign second of time
they move deeply
into the hidden realms
of the city
their lights
caress my eyes

twenty

a man
a Tokyo man stands
    he stands
    hanging one
    on the side of the
    deserting street

a lady
a Tokyo lady stands
    she is waiting
    awaiting something
    I know not what

the neon lights
reflect off of both of their skins
    displaying
    decaying
    telling a story
    that can never be fathomed
    never be truly understood
        only seen
        only witnessed

    he is dressed in gray pants
    a dark blue jacket
    his eyes are hidden deeply
    into the pole
    where he has made his perch

she has long black hair
a long black coat
her eyes
stare into some distance
that my western eyes
will never see

I pass him
I pass her
he is vacant
his back is turned to me
her face
radiates the reflecting colors
pink
red
blue
all of the Tokyo night

him
I have no feelings for

her
I could love
given the chance

pictures and scenes
and all the figures in a dream

they all add up
to the same thing

nothing
not anything at all

twenty-one

the night
is still young
the feeling
is still strong

everywhere to go
everywhere to run

placid
drunken
enlightenment

based in a fool's desire
of a fool's dream
of a fool's journey
into a drunken
fool's night

twenty-two

now
I walk past the loft
of my Tokyo dreams

    heavy metal
    new wave
    punk rock
    queen

the years
yes
they have gone by

it was another night
another life
another time

    time
    a time ago

and she whispers to me
yes
she lied to me
her words
they merged with silence

    the nighttime
    it is for whispers
    the daytime

it is for screams
but her nighttime
is what I remember
the nighttime
a long time ago

and in all that has been found
since
and all that is eternally lost
her kiss
it remains
in my pages of memories
memories
yes
memories
of a time
a long time ago

gray life
and black hair dyed blue
ancient wisdom
Asian kiss
the lost
loving
and lonely touch
of her momentary love
in a momentary life
time
a long time ago

twenty-three

there is a family market
open by the loft
the loft
at 1:00 AM

orange lights glow
into the night
spraying the distance
with drunken illustrations of suchness

        what are they doing
                the people still inside

        what are they doing
                the illuminations
        that spread false glory
        over the hallowedness
        of the dark

        what are they doing

        what am I doing

        who shall it be
        that every truly knows

twenty-four

a drunken businessman
staggers in front of me

        his world turns
        my world turns
                spinning
                on-and-on

he fades to the left
I fade to the right

somehow
like the continual movement
of the hands of a clock
our wavering movements
support one another
and the world
it all seems aligned

twenty-five

hello
whore who stokes the night
        move
        and
        groove

awaiting the coming passion
you sit silently
in a darkened park

does my golden blonde presence
startle you
does it make you want to squirm

am I so different
than those before me
so different
from those that will later come

        yes
        I know
        this is
        Tokyo
        yes
        I know
        the sun
        has set
        long ago
        yes

I know
I am the only one
of my race
stalking this pagan night
yes
I know
I want you too

stumble at my sight
rose from the rail
upon which you sit
move away
to another
on coming figure
with eyes similar to your own

you could have me
you could have him
the price
it would be the same

but the body
of love
the blood
of lust
it speaks
in a foreign tongue

I speak it
you say it
I feel it
you know it
can anything mean
anything more

but you ran away
from this distant touch
fear
it should not live
in the heart
of a whore

but all promises
are made
few
are ever kept
and the easy way out
leads to the
easy way in
it leads to something
something
like nothing before

so run
I say to you goodbye
I say it in your native tongue

surprise
you could have had me
surprise
I speak your language

twenty-six

it is dark
yes
I know
the world
it is dark
it may ways unseen

the night howls
in all of its fear
I touch it
I like it
yes
I want it
this way

a park
where the night dwellers
come out to play

and you know
if you want to play
you have to pay

a park
it is dark
inhabited by those
who in the day
during the day

I would have
nothing to say

but this is the dream
yes
this is the lie
only to be known
by one
by one by two or by three

those of the other kind
the other kind
that of which
I am not one
    the safe
    the sound
    the faithful
    the holy
    those with something
    left to lose

    leave them to their day
    for I will take the night

    stroke me
    stroke me

it is dark now
yes
I know

it is late
yes
I know that too

maybe too late
for all those for sale
they look to have been taken
all those who run free
they look to be gone
all those who are nothing(s)
they are nowhere in sight

the last one
on the chopping block
she was just stolen
from the reach
of my grasp

twenty-seven

I hear people talking
men in the night
they yell something at me
something
I do not understand

"Fuck you!"
I say

"Do you understand me?"

maybe this is your world
maybe this city
belongs to you
maybe this country is your own
but the night
it belongs to me

"Fuck you!"

twenty-eight

a candy man comes up to me
he grabs hold
hands on his crouch
he wants to know
do I want some
some of what he has to sell
a woman
hidden somewhere
deeply
out of sight.

now I always have been one to feel
I always seem to know
what's *comein'* down
long before it ever does

this time
though the temptation
grabs a hard hold of me
it is just my felling(s)
to walk on
walk away

    thanks a lot dude
    next time around

me
I prefer the chase

the desire
the tracking it down

me
I want the play
I don’t want a pimp’s knife
in my back
as I am *a-getting’* my love *thAng* on

    thanks a lot dude
    next time around

twenty-nine

someone just bowed to me
as they re-entered
the door
to their abode

late night/all night
positive passion
they
like me
formal
to the end

caressed ancient goddess
caressed ancient myth
you look at me
I look at you
a bow
a bow in return

yes
it is the late night
no
there is no reason
for anything at all
yes
we see the passion
no
it cannot be ours to hold

so we fade
to temporal memory
sleep and dreams
they are allowed to be known

all is held
all is understood
all is felt
in a fleeting moment
when a beautiful stranger
the embodiment of the goddess
bows to me
I bow to her

it could have been anyone
for it did not need to happen at all
but it did happen
          happen
          it was known
          happen
          it was felt

may the bow
go on forever

thirty

I stagger drunkenly
through the whore section
of TKO: (Tokyo)

sober
it is closing in on me
far too fast

soapland
I could go
but I know
the women who walk the streets
have so much more
to offer me

    love and lust
    pain and disease
        poetry all the same

    kiss and tell
    sins and hell
        a reason by any other name

for in this world
of the streets
you know
that I am home

the streets
they are all
that I have ever known

    no
    this is not Bangkok
        for it is far too clean
    no
    this is not Shanghai
        for here
        there is no woman
        waiting for me
    no
    this is not Hong Kong
        it would be simple
        if it were
    this is Tokyo
    this is the night
    and I want it hard
    I want it hard and heavy
    with a glare of anger
    in a whore's screaming eyes

the streets
I think that they are too clean
I think that they are too lost
    even for me

inside
it is all too much inside

inside
is never
outside

inside
never holds the keys
to the street

inside
it is for the faithful
not the faithless
inside
it is for the introvert
        not the screamers
        that hold the passages
        to the places
        of the warriors
        of the night

thirty-one

the night comes on
like some lonesome leech in heat

god, I hate to sober up
I prefer the haze
that is the product of the drink

I walk
with my California strut
no women
        and my dick
        it is still in hock

I hear showers
they take place around me
naked flesh
cleansing itself for the bounds of love
water running down
lovers intertwined
beds move
magic as always
is all that is promised
        promised
        but rarely magic is fulfilled

the night
I hear it
it promises all

but I
I still walk alone

would it better
had I never heard these sounds
would it be better
had I never known the feeling

better
yes
easier
no

but every poet
they must know the score
every player
plays the game

a soft and flowing art piece
it covers the dark blue
covers
the Tokyo sky

I look to it
for answers
I try to understand
its reasons

it is
what it is

I am
what I am

the sounds
the colors
the feelings
they are all my embrace

they kiss me
and all I can do
is return their touch

thirty-two

looking for lust
the passion of reason
looking for love
by any other name

I touch the night
with the best of *'em*
I control it
it is mine
it is what I am

I hold it
it controls me
who is the victor
who is in command

the passive
they are packing it in
the passionate
have no room for surrender

    no room for surrender
    no room for defeat

what isn't here today
I will create tomorrow
I do not live life
I attack it

thirty-three

all this drunken stupor
simply reaffirms what I am

I hold onto the top handrail
more or less it is a bar

        the Japanese
        well
        hey
        their handrails
        they are several inches
        maybe a foot
        below what I find necessary
                but each person is
                as each person does

I take hold
it helps me remain
in formation position
        straight up
as I walk home
home alone
back to my five star hotel
that touches the stars
in the sky

        now I was a drunk
        as the best of *'em*

sobering slowly
into the reality
of the known lie

but my hair
it is not short
it is long
my hair
it is not black
it is blonde

and my eyes
they are not brown
they are blue

so perhaps
this night
illustrates all that is
in this land
the land of the rising sun

as fool's dream
in a fool's lie

this night
it grows old
old and alone

I could not find

flesh fulfillment
not even in the hands
of a fleeting whore
        who walked the park
        in the pagan night

        your loss, baby
        your loss

        but
        I would have love to love
        your love
        your love
        that burns this night black

                black
                like your hair
                black
                like your eyes
                black
                like your heart
                your heart
                and my heart

        I would have loved to have loved
        your love

        your love
        you fading whore
        in an aging night

it is your loss
the love
my love
love
which you will never know

so perhaps
I am saved
from dreaded diseases
perhaps this poetry
of aloneness
alienation
from the arms of a whore
in a dreamer's blatant reality
has thus
become real

perhaps these words
may now be cast
to the ages
and perhaps
my going home alone
is the duty paid
for these word's written
in a land of plenty

perhaps
I do not know

it is all too complex
for me

so as my poetry
is redundant
as all poetry is
and as my life
hangs in the balance
of twenty-nine years old
and as my love
well
it never has been
fully fulfilled

it keeps me dreaming
it keeps me wanting
it keeps me desiring
it keeps me trying

the food
for all the poetry of redundancy

so sing to me
of your mystic rhythms
as the Tokyo traffic
breathes on

and there are the masses
and there are the chances
but the nighttime
it makes them all calm down

as I walk on
into the nighttime

distance
may separate us all

I see my hotel
towering
in its enormity
there it is
firm and still

I see lights
some
they are still on
        lights and lies
        how the cry
        distance
        into the abstraction
        of the fading night

and as the transcribers find
the truth
in all that is written
as the readers find
what is hidden
deeply between the lines
as the cries
and the lies
the dream
and the screams
they call out their woes to me
as I walk
dead center
dead on
dead drunk
into the failing embrace
of this Tokyo night

thirty-four

suits and ties
how they lie
as they caress
every woman's
dreaming soul

truth equals lies
lies equal truth
you know
what that means
to the true sportsman
the dreamers
lost in the night

promises of external vision
how they never hold the truth

> life it lives
> life it dies
> what falls in between
> is all our creation

so I hold onto the art
art
for lack of any better word
I hold on
to all that I am
nothing that the mindless masses
could ever/would ever find acceptable

so give me a dream
worth believing
please give me another lie
give me anything
but what already is
I'll take the fool's illusion
any day

glowing red
and glowing amber
sing to me
sing to me

for I have
nothing left to lose

I stroke this Tokyo night
as it strokes me
I stoke anyone of the illusions
I stroke anyone of the rejections
rejections
and walking

so I walk to a restaurant
twenty-four hours a day

to my right hand
lives my illusion

my bed it waits
lonely for me

people come upon me
I see them
they see me
glances in the haze
visions in the night

and every vision
is another lie

Thirty-five

love
I walk home
2:00 AM
maybe three
I hope
I am sober enough
not to have a kill hangover
tomorrow morning

I still stagger a bit

god
it is fucking cold

I went into a restaurant
had a club sandwich
or at least
Tokyo's interpretation of the same
I had a couple cups
of the java
now I can go
to my hotel room suite
dose down a couple of alka-seltzers
a couple of aspirins on the side

a couple hours of the Z's
and who knows
what tomorrow may bring

thirty-six

I pass a group
of drunken teenagers
speaking the few a words
of English
that they know
to me

saying,
"Have a good dream."

well
that I have had
that I continue to have

dream
dream forever

thirty-seven

well…
I ride up in the elevator
my California driver's license
my money
my rubbers
still intact

14
15
16
17…

I suppose
that I am glad
in some foolish way
that I did not end my night
in the arms of a whore
who has known so many before
just like me
known so many
so many unknowables
long ago I forgot their names
if I ever even knew them
but now
I begin to forget their faces
and to me
that is sad

I suppose
that I am glad
        I suppose
        or I suppose not

the question of destiny
it lives
it breathes
        in my mind
it answers
only to its own destiny
and it tries to force it
down the throat of mine

a fool's illusion
by any other name

21
22
23
24…

what a dream
what an illusion

        have a good dream
                is what they said to me

a dream
that lasts forever
a dream
that never was
a dream
that has fallen asleep
too easy
a dream…

the joke is on me

30
31
32

34

38…

the floor bell chimes
the night sings
of its fading glory
to me

I walk down the hall
to my room
alone

thirty-eight

here I am
this drunken poet
looking
out onto
this Tokyo night

I wonder
where I have gone wrong
why
I am haunted
haunted by the mystery
hunted by the misery
pursued by the lies

I look out onto
this Tokyo night
like so many times before

like so many others have
but so few have truly known

I look out
this Tokyo night
and I scream
and I yell
and I wonder why

why
this drunken poet
with the poetry of the ages
having sung through my veins
I wonder why
this drunken poet
is one again
alone

is alone
all that matters
to a poet's life
is that where all
the messages/the inspirations
come from
it must be

for so many poets
have cried

so I look into the mirror
the mirror
of longing woes
and I see myself
I see myself as I speak
I see myself as I write

and it all is
as it should be

as I have said
time and time before

but time and time before
they are all but lies

as the lies are spoken in truth
as the lies become the truth
and as all lies
are as I
alone
lost
separated

and so
just as all
the longing nighttime lingerers
I go to bed
alone

I scratch the beard
growing along my face
I push back my long blonde hair

it is all I
all I
in a Tokyo night

a night
that has been driven
and drunken

a night
that did not have to be

but a night
that I have chosen to live

and as every mistral sings
sings and plays
with the lute of ages
and as every poet dreams
every poet wishes
for the love of ages

so I have danced
I have sung
I have tired
tried so hard
        god
        I have tried so hard
        but I have ended up
                here
                alone

perhaps that is what makes me the poet
the poet that I am

so
good night

S.
13 October 1987
Tokyo, Japan

About the Author

Scott Shaw is a prolific author, actor, filmmaker, and musician. Throughout his life, Shaw has continually returned to Asia, documenting obscure aspects of Asian culture in words and on film. He is a frequently featured contributor to Martial and Meditative Art Journals and is the author of numerous books on Modern Literature, Poetry, Asian Culture, the Martial Arts, Zen Buddhism, Yoga, and Meditation.

Scott Shaw's *Books-In-Print* include:

The Little Book of Yoga Breathing,
Nirvana in a Nutshell,
About Peace: 108 Ways to Be At Peace
When Things Are Out of Control,
Zen O'clock: Time To Be,
The Tao of Self Defense,
Samurai Zen,
The Ki Process: Korean Secrets
for Cultivating Dynamic Energy,
The Warrior is Silent:
Martial Arts and the Spiritual Path,
Hapkido: The Korean Art of Self Defense,
Hapkido: Essays on Self-Defense,
Taekwondo Basics,
Advanced Taekwondo,
Bangkok and the Nights of Drunken Stupor,
Chi Kung For Beginners,
Mastering Health: The A to Z of Chi Kung,
Cambodia Refugees in Long Beach, California,
China Deep,
Essence: The Zen of Everything,
Scream: Southeast Asia and the Dream,
Shanghai Whispers Shanghai Screams,
Shattered Thoughts,
Junk: The Back Streets of Bangkok,
The Passionate Kiss of Illusion,
TKO: Lost Nights in Tokyo,
Zen Buddhism: The Pathway to Nirvana,
Zen: Tales from the Journey,
Zen in the Blink of an Eye,
Yoga: A Spiritual Guidebook,
Marguerite Duras and Charles Bukowski: The Yin
and Yang of Modern Erotic Literature.

www.ingramcontent.com/pod-product-compliance
Lightning Source LLC
LaVergne TN
LVHW020653100826
845148LV00012B/2474

9781877792083